PREPARATORY SET #2

RUDIMENTS EXAM SERIES

By Glory St. Germain ARCT RMT MYCC UMTC &
Shelagh McKibbon-U'Ren RMT UMTC

ULTIMATE
MUSIC THEORY

GSG MUSIC

Enriching Lives Through Music Education

ISBN: 978-1-927641-01-9

The Ultimate Music Theory™ Program
Enriching Lives Through Music Education

The Ultimate Music Theory™ Workbooks & Answer Books Program includes:

UMT Rudiments Workbooks for Prep 1, Prep 2, Basic, Intermediate, Advanced & Complete
UMT Exam Series (Set #1 & Set #2) for Preparatory, Basic, Intermediate & Advanced

Supplemental Workbooks for PREP LEVEL, LEVELS 1 - 8 & COMPLETE LEVEL
UMT Supplemental Exam Series for LEVEL 5, LEVEL 6, LEVEL 7 & LEVEL 8

The Ultimate Music Theory Program is the *Way to Score Success* as UMT helps students prepare for nationally recognized theory examinations including the Royal Conservatory of Music.

 Library and Archives Canada Cataloguing in Publication. UMT Workbooks & Exam Series /Glory St. Germain & Shelagh McKibbon-U'Ren. Respect Copyright. All rights reserved. GlorylandPublishing.com

Ultimate Music Theory Rudiments Exam Series

GP - EPS1	ISBN: 978-1-927641-00-2	Preparatory Rudiments Exams Set #1
GP - EPS1A	ISBN: 978-1-927641-08-8	Preparatory Exams Answers Set #1
GP - EPS2	ISBN: 978-1-927641-01-9	Preparatory Rudiments Exams Set #2
GP - EPS2A	ISBN: 978-1-927641-09-5	Preparatory Exams Answers Set #2
GP - EBS1	ISBN: 978-1-927641-02-6	Basic Rudiments Exams Set #1
GP - EBS1A	ISBN: 978-1-927641-10-1	Basic Exams Answers Set #1
GP - EBS2	ISBN: 978-1-927641-03-3	Basic Rudiments Exams Set #2
GP - EBS2A	ISBN: 978-1-927641-11-8	Basic Exams Answers Set #2
GP - EIS1	ISBN: 978-1-927641-04-0	Intermediate Rudiments Exams Set #1
GP - EIS1A	ISBN: 978-1-927641-12-5	Intermediate Exams Answers Set #1
GP - EIS2	ISBN: 978-1-927641-05-7	Intermediate Rudiments Exams Set #2
GP - EIS2A	ISBN: 978-1-927641-13-2	Intermediate Exams Answers Set #2
GP - EAS1	ISBN: 978-1-927641-06-4	Advanced Rudiments Exams Set #1
GP - EAS1A	ISBN: 978-1-927641-14-9	Advanced Exams Answers Set #1
GP - EAS2	ISBN: 978-1-927641-07-1	Advanced Rudiments Exams Set #2
GP - EAS2A	ISBN: 978-1-927641-15-6	Advanced Exams Answers Set #2

Ultimate Music Theory Supplemental Exam Series

GP-L5E	ISBN: 978-1-990358-11-1	LEVEL 5 Exams
GP-L5EA	ISBN: 978-1-990358-12-8	LEVEL 5 Exams Answers
GP-L6E	ISBN: 978-1-990358-13-5	LEVEL 6 Exams
GP-L6EA	ISBN: 978-1-990358-14-2	LEVEL 6 Exams Answers
GP-L7E	ISBN: 978-1-990358-15-9	LEVEL 7 Exams
GP-L7EA	ISBN: 978-1-990358-16-6	LEVEL 7 Exams Answers
GP-L8E	ISBN: 978-1-990358-17-3	LEVEL 8 Exams
GP-L8EA	ISBN: 978-1-990358-18-0	LEVEL 8 Exams Answers

Go to UltimateMusicTheory.com **and check out the FREE Resources**

Ultimate Music Theory FREE RESOURCES created just for you!

The **Ultimate Music Theory Exams** reinforce the **UMT Prep 1 and Prep 2 Rudiments Workbooks** and prepare students for continued learning with UMT Basic Rudiments.

Preparatory Rudiments Theory Examination requirements are:

Pitch
- Grand Staff (Treble Clef or G Clef and Bass Clef or F Clef)
- Note names (up to two ledger lines below and above the Treble Clef and Bass Clef)
- Accidentals (sharp, flat and natural signs)
- Whole tones (whole steps) and semitones (half steps)
- Matching notes to the corresponding keys on the keyboard
- Naming or drawing notes on the staff that are shown on a keyboard

Rhythm
- Note and rest time values (whole, half, quarter and eighth)
- Dotted half notes and dotted quarter notes
- Adding Time Signatures, bar lines and rests to a given line of music
- Simple Time Signatures ($\frac{2}{4}$, $\frac{3}{4}$, $\frac{4}{4}$, and **C**)

Scales in the keys of C Major, G Major and F Major
- Write or identify: Scales, ascending or descending, one octave
- Key Signatures
- Tonic scale degree

Triads in the keys of C Major, G Major and F Major
- Write or identify: Solid (blocked) in Root Position, beginning on the Tonic note (with or without a Key Signature)
- Identify: Broken in Root Position, beginning on the Tonic note (with or without a Key Signature)

Intervals
- Write or identify: above a given note, all intervals up to and including an octave (numerical size only), melodic or harmonic
- Identify: below a given note, all intervals up to and including an octave (numerical size only), melodic form only

Musical Terms and Signs
- Recognize, define or supply the musical terms or signs as listed in the Prep 1 and Prep 2 Ultimate Music Theory Workbooks

Analysis
- Analyze a short musical composition, identifying any of the above theory requirements

Score:
60 - 69 Pass; **70 - 79** Honors; **80 - 89** First Class Honors; **90 - 100** First Class Honors with Distinction

Ultimate Music Theory: *The Way to Score Success!*

UltimateMusicTheory.com © Copyright 2013 Gloryland Publishing. All Rights Reserved.

ULTIMATE MUSIC THEORY
PREPARATORY EXAM SET #2 - EXAM #1

Total Score: ___
100

> ♪ **UMT Tip:** Middle C can be written in the Treble Clef or in the Bass Clef. Notes above (to the right on the keyboard) of Middle C will be written in the Treble Clef. Notes below (to the left on the keyboard) of Middle C will be written in the Bass Clef.

1. a) Write the notes on the Grand Staff for the keys marked with a ☺. Use whole notes.
   b) Name the notes.
   c) Draw a line from each note to the corresponding key on the keyboard (at the correct pitch).

   /10

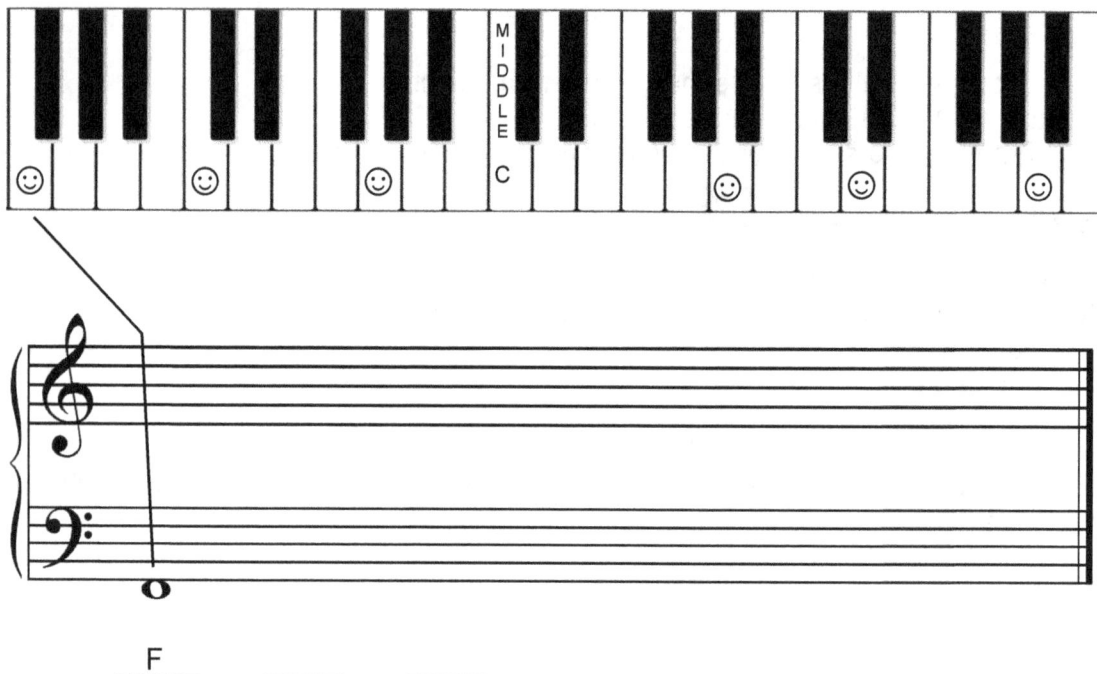

F ___ ___ ___ ___ ___

> ♪ **UMT Tip:** A Key Signature affects all the notes on the staff (and on ledger lines) with the same letter name.

1. d) Name the following notes. (Observe the Key Signature.)

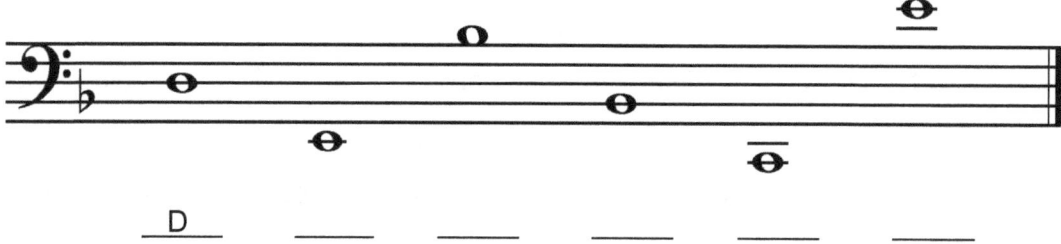

D ___ ___ ___ ___ ___

UltimateMusicTheory.com © Copyright 2013 Gloryland Publishing. All Rights Reserved.

ULTIMATE MUSIC THEORY
PREPARATORY EXAM SET #2 - EXAM #1

> ♪ **UMT Tip:** When writing the note one semitone above a given note using the same letter name, accidentals will be used to raise the given note.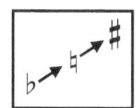

2. a) Write the note that is one semitone above each of the given notes. Use the same letter name. Use whole notes. Name both notes.

10

   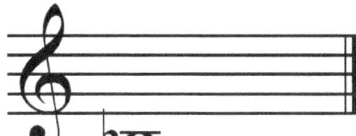

_____   _____

   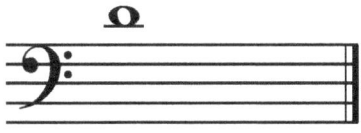   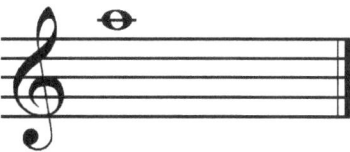

_____   _____   _____

> ♪ **UMT Tip:** When writing the note one semitone below a given note using the same letter name, accidentals will be used to lower the given note.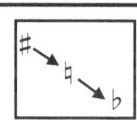

b) Write the note that is one semitone below each of the given notes. Use the same letter name. Use whole notes. Name both notes.

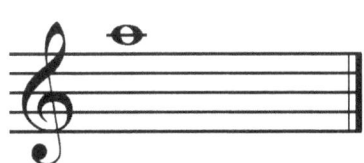      

_____   _____   _____

   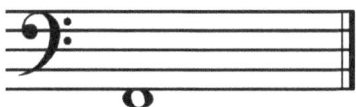

_____   _____

UltimateMusicTheory.com © Copyright 2013 Gloryland Publishing. All Rights Reserved.

ULTIMATE MUSIC THEORY
PREPARATORY EXAM SET #2 - EXAM #1

> ♪ **UMT Tip:** When naming the interval (number size only), always count from the bottom (lower) note to the top (higher) note. Accidentals do not affect the number size of the interval.

3. Name each of the following intervals. (Write the number size only.)

> ♪ **UMT Tip:** When writing the note a whole tone (whole step) above a note, use neighbouring (next-door) letter names. Write the notes separately (one note after the other). Draw a small keyboard to help you find the correct notes.

4. Write the note that is a whole tone above each given note. Use whole notes.

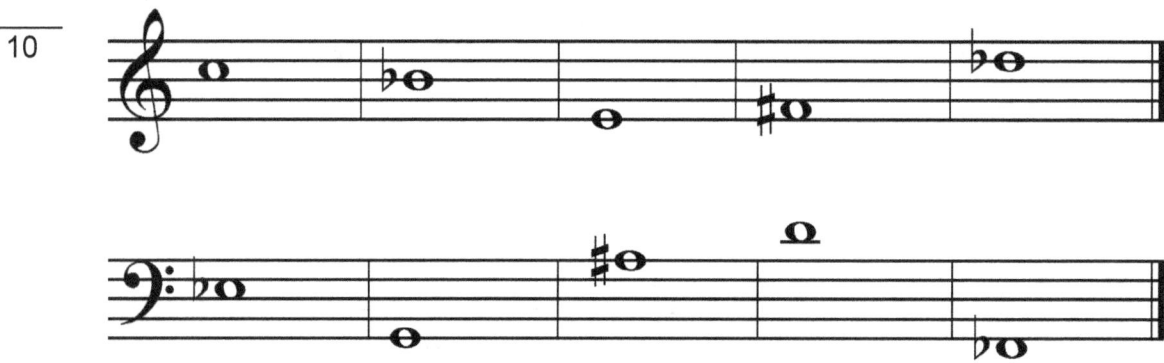

UltimateMusicTheory.com © Copyright 2013 Gloryland Publishing. All Rights Reserved.

ULTIMATE MUSIC THEORY
PREPARATORY EXAM SET #2 - EXAM #1

> ♪ **UMT Tip:** When writing a scale going up or down one octave, the Tonic note is the first note and the last (final) note. The Roman Numeral "I" is used to label the Tonic note.

5. a) Write the scale of F Major, descending (going down) one octave. Use accidentals instead of a Key Signature. Use whole notes. Circle two Tonic notes. Label them **I**.

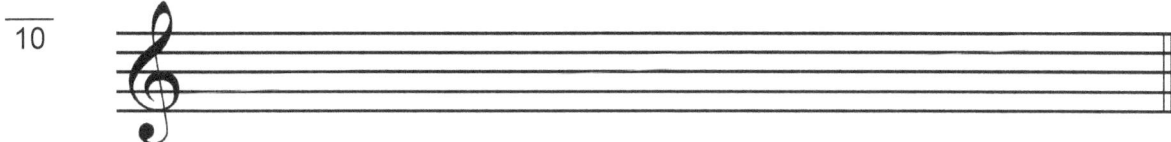

b) Write the scale of G Major, ascending (going up) one octave. Use accidentals instead of a Key Signature. Use whole notes. Circle two Tonic notes. Label them **I**.

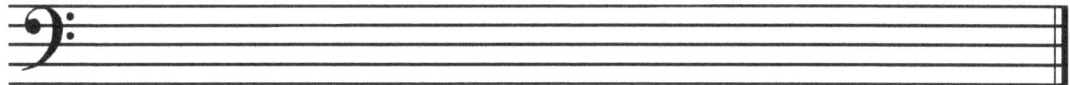

c) Add a Treble Clef or a Bass Clef at the beginning of the following staff to form the C Major Scale (ascending).

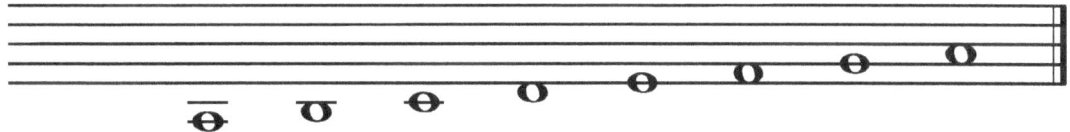

d) Write the Key Signature and the Tonic note for each of the following keys. Use whole notes.

F Major   G Major

G Major   C Major

UltimateMusicTheory.com © Copyright 2013 Gloryland Publishing. All Rights Reserved.

ULTIMATE MUSIC THEORY
PREPARATORY EXAM SET #2 - EXAM #1

> ♪ **UMT Tip:** A solid (blocked) triad is written one note above the other (together; all 3 notes on lines or all 3 notes in spaces). The root note is the bottom (lowest) note.
> A broken triad is written one note after the other (separately; all 3 notes on lines or all 3 notes in spaces). The root note is the bottom (lowest) note.

6. a) Identify the root note of each triad.
   b) Circle whether the triad is Solid or Broken.

[10]

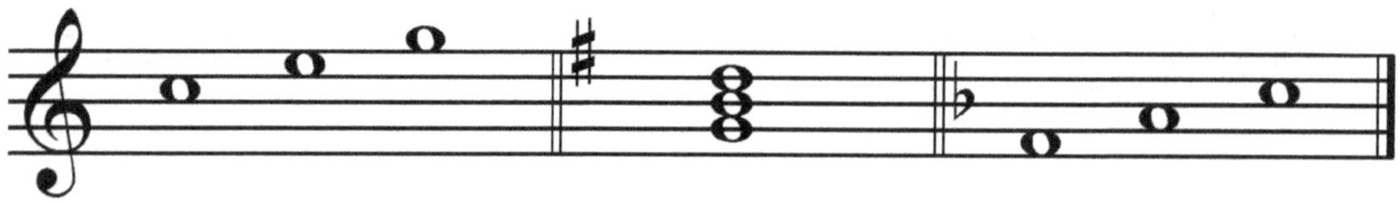

a) Root: _____   Root: _____   Root: _____

b) Solid   Solid   Solid

   Broken   Broken   Broken

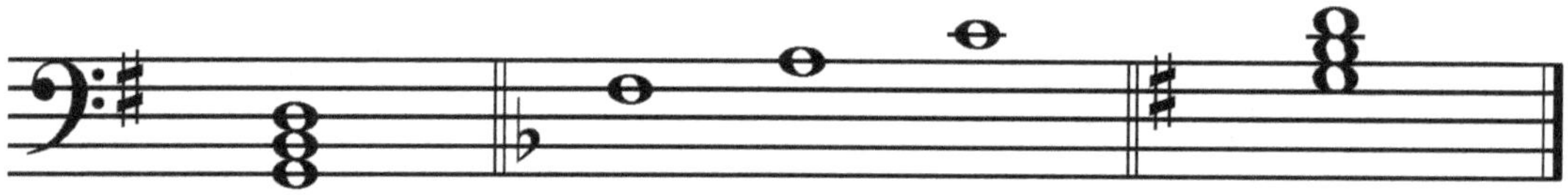

a) Root: _____   Root: _____   Root: _____

b) Solid   Solid   Solid

   Broken   Broken   Broken

a) Root: _____   Root: _____   Root: _____   Root: _____

b) Solid   Solid   Solid   Solid

   Broken   Broken   Broken   Broken

UltimateMusicTheory.com © Copyright 2013 Gloryland Publishing. All Rights Reserved.

ULTIMATE MUSIC THEORY
PREPARATORY EXAM SET #2 - EXAM #1

> ♪ **UMT Tip:** In 4/4 time, a quarter note equals one count.

7. a) Name the type of rests. Indicate the number of counts each rest receives in 4/4 time.

Rest: _____ _____ _____ _____

Count: _____ _____ _____ _____

b) Name the type of notes. Indicate the number of counts each note receives in 4/4 time.

Note: _____ _____ _____

Count: _____ _____ _____

Note: _____ _____ _____

Count: _____ _____ _____

UltimateMusicTheory.com © Copyright 2013 Gloryland Publishing. All Rights Reserved.

ULTIMATE MUSIC THEORY
PREPARATORY EXAM SET #2 - EXAM #1

> ♪ **UMT Tip:** 𝄴 is known as Common Time. It is the same as $\frac{4}{4}$.

8. a) Add bar lines to complete the following rhythms.

> ♪ **UMT Tip:** A whole rest is used for a whole measure of silence.

b) Add rests below each bracket to complete each measure.

ULTIMATE MUSIC THEORY
PREPARATORY EXAM SET #2 - EXAM #1

> ♪ **UMT Tip:** Before looking at the possible definitions, look at the Term and identify the definition. Then match the definition with one of the given definitions.

9. Match each musical term with its English definition. (Not all definitions will be used.)

Term		Definition
a tempo	_____	a) very slow
legato	_____	b) fast
staccato	_____	c) at a moderate tempo
ritardando, rit.	_____	d) cancels a sharp or a flat
allegro	_____	e) return to the original tempo
diminuendo, dim.	_____	f) moderately slow; at a walking pace
largo	_____	g) smooth
crescendo, cresc.	_____	h) slowing down gradually
moderato	_____	i) detached
andante	_____	j) becoming softer
		k) becoming louder

___
10

ULTIMATE MUSIC THEORY
PREPARATORY EXAM SET #2 - EXAM #1

♪ **UMT Tip:** The root of a triad is the lower (bottom) note of the triad.

10. Analyze the following excerpt of music by answering the questions below.

Minuet and Trio

Andante
Ludwig van Beethoven

a) Name the title of this excerpt. _____

b) Name the composer of this excerpt. _____

c) Add the Time Signature directly on the music.

d) How many counts does the rest at the letter **A** receive? _____

e) Name the notes at the letters **B**: _____ **C**: _____

f) Name the interval at **D** (number size only). _____

g) Circle the name of the rest at the letter **E**.   Eighth   Quarter   Half

h) Find a Tonic triad of G Major in this excerpt and circle it. Label it G Maj.

i) How many times does the note F♯ appear in this excerpt? _____

j) How many slurs are in this excerpt? _____

ULTIMATE MUSIC THEORY
PREPARATORY EXAM SET #2 - EXAM #2

Total Score: ___ / 100

1. a) Name the following notes.
    b) Draw a line from each note to the corresponding key on the keyboard (at the correct pitch).

___/10

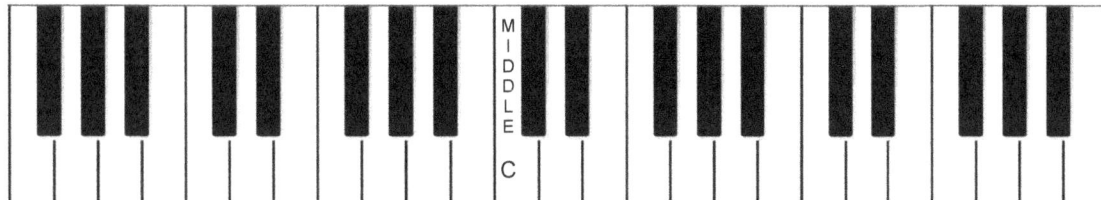

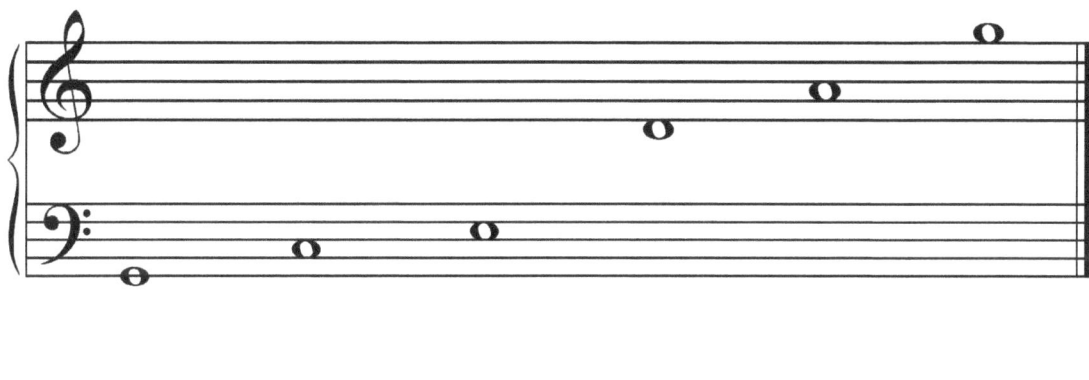

___ ___ ___ ___ ___

c) Write the following notes in the Treble Clef. Use half notes.

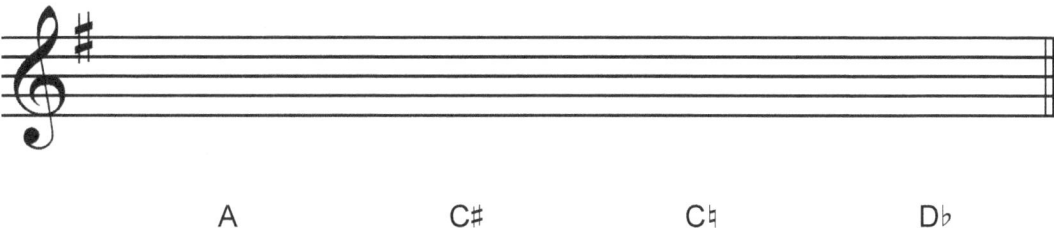

UltimateMusicTheory.com © Copyright 2013 Gloryland Publishing. All Rights Reserved.

ULTIMATE MUSIC THEORY
PREPARATORY EXAM SET #2 - EXAM #2

2. a) For each pair of notes, circle the note which sounds lower in pitch. Name the notes.

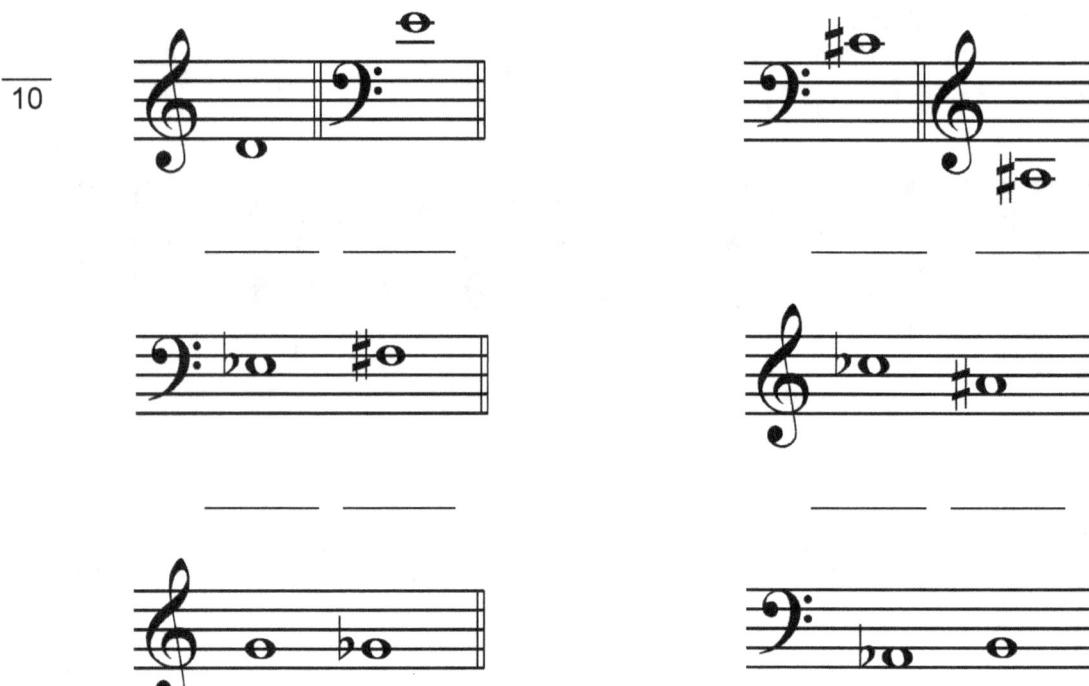

b) Indicate whether the distance between the notes in each measure is a semitone (half step) or a whole tone (whole step) by circling either SEMITONE or WHOLE TONE.

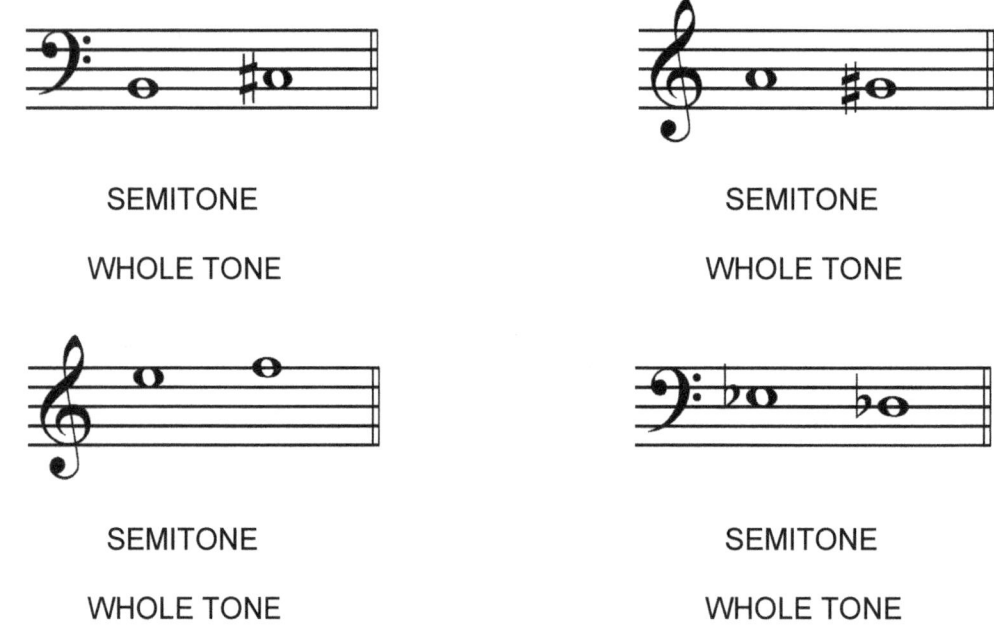

SEMITONE

WHOLE TONE

SEMITONE

WHOLE TONE

SEMITONE

WHOLE TONE

SEMITONE

WHOLE TONE

ULTIMATE MUSIC THEORY
PREPARATORY EXAM SET #2 - EXAM #2

3. a) Name each of the following melodic intervals. (Write the number size only.)

[10]

b) Write a note above each of the given notes to form the following harmonic intervals. Use whole notes.

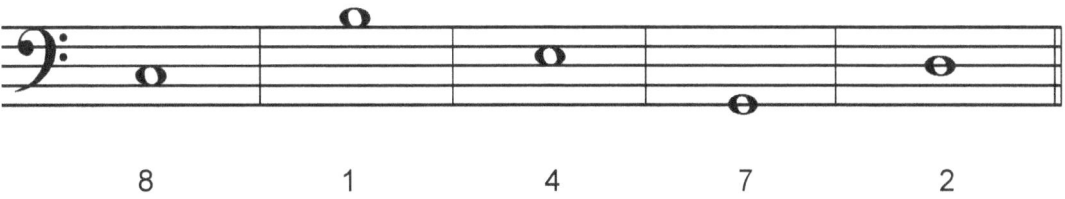

4. Add rests below each bracket to complete each measure.

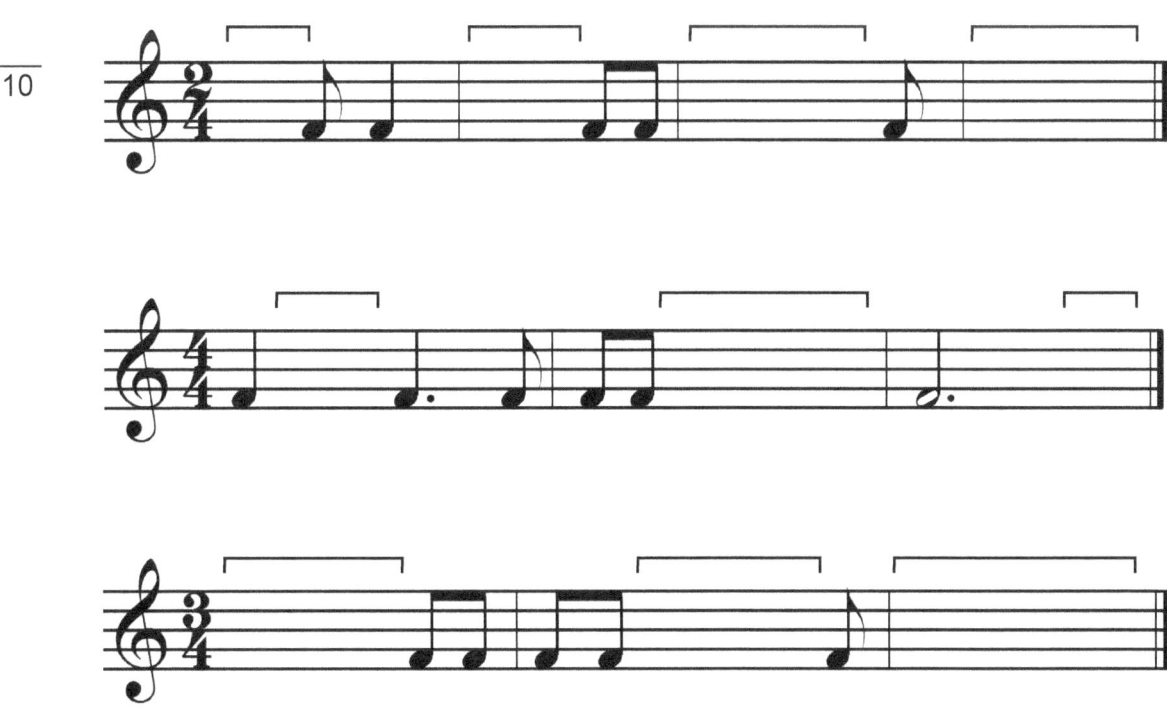

[10]

ULTIMATE MUSIC THEORY
PREPARATORY EXAM SET #2 - EXAM #2

5. a) Identify the following scales as C major, F Major or G Major.
    b) In each scale, circle one Tonic note. Label it as I.

Scale: _____

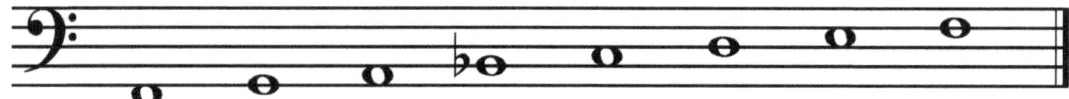

Scale: _____

Scale: _____

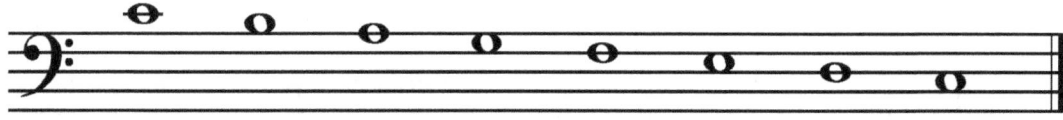

Scale: _____

ULTIMATE MUSIC THEORY
PREPARATORY EXAM SET #2 - EXAM #2

6. Match each triad name with the correct triad.

___
10

G Major Triad, Broken, _____   a)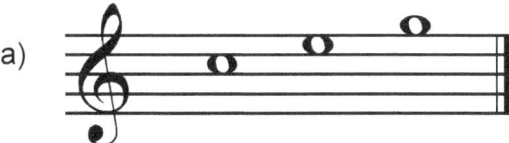
in the Treble Clef

F Major Triad, Solid, _____   b)
in the Treble Clef

C Major Triad, Solid, _____   c)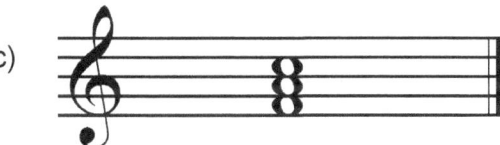
in the Bass Clef

C Major Triad, Broken, _____   d)
in the Treble Clef

G Major Triad, Solid, _____   e)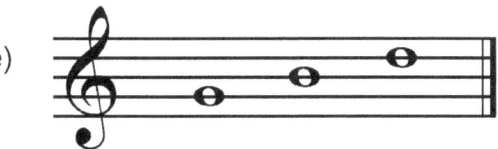
in the Bass Clef

ULTIMATE MUSIC THEORY
PREPARATORY EXAM SET #2 - EXAM #2

7. a) Name each of the following rests. Do not use abbreviations.

10

▬ = _____

▬. = _____

𝄽 = _____

𝄾 = _____

b) Draw an example of each of the following notes. Observe the stem direction.

a quarter note (stem pointing down) = _____

a single eighth note (stem pointing up) = _____

a dotted half note (stem pointing down) = _____

a single eighth note (stem pointing down) = _____

a dotted quarter note (stem pointing up) = _____

two eighth notes joined with a beam (stems = _____
pointing down)

UltimateMusicTheory.com © Copyright 2013 Gloryland Publishing. All Rights Reserved.

ULTIMATE MUSIC THEORY
PREPARATORY EXAM SET #2 - EXAM #2

8. a) Add bar lines to complete the following rhythms.

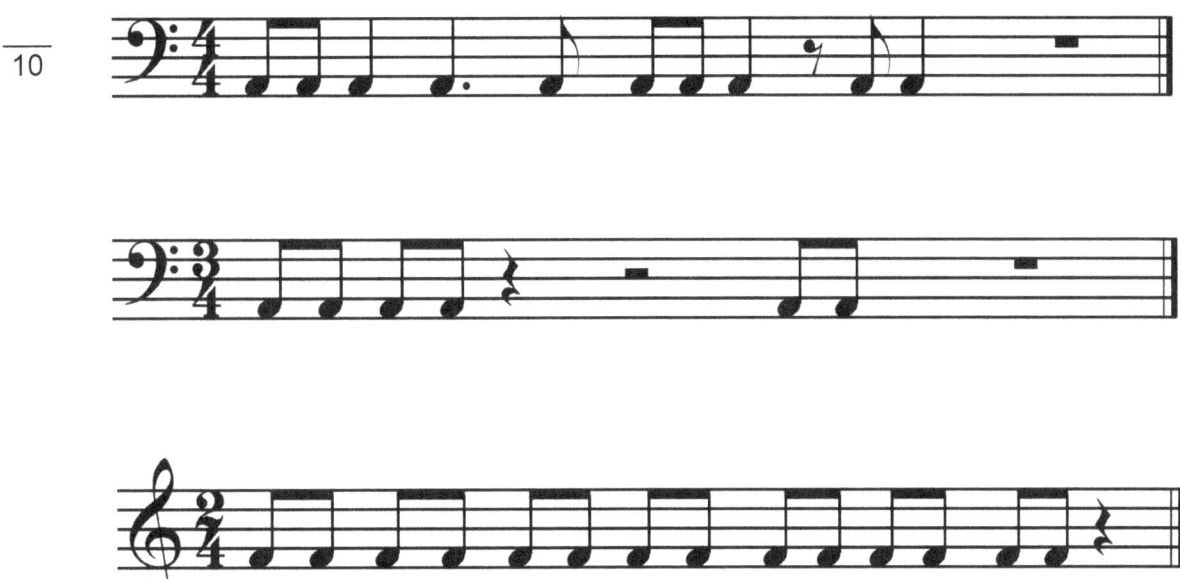

b) Add the correct Time Signature below each bracket.

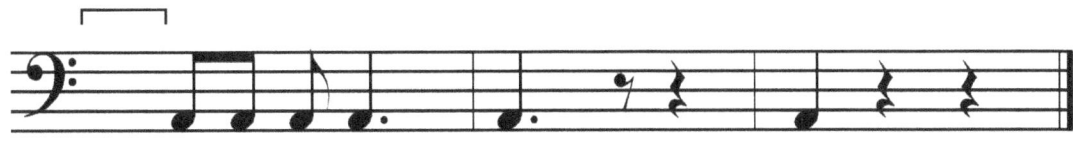

ULTIMATE MUSIC THEORY
PREPARATORY EXAM SET #2 - EXAM #2

9. Write the correct Italian term for the following definitions. Do not use signs or abbreviations.

Definition	Italian Term
soft	_____
at a moderate tempo	_____
becoming louder	_____
detached	_____
medium loud	_____
smooth	_____
very slow	_____
slowing down gradually	_____
return to the original tempo	_____
moderately slow; at a walking pace	_____

ULTIMATE MUSIC THEORY
PREPARATORY EXAM SET #2 - EXAM #2

10. Analyze the following piece of music by answering the questions below.

a) Name the title of this piece. _____

b) Explain the tempo of this piece. _____

c) Add the Time Signature directly on the music.

e) Add a dynamic sign in measure 1 that indicates to play loud (forte).

d) Name the notes at the letters **A**: _____ **B**: _____

f) Add dots to the notes in the Bass Clef at measure 2 to create staccato quarter notes.

g) Explain the signs at **C** and **D**. _____

h) Add the missing rest in measure 4 at **E**.

i) Name the rest in measure 4 at **F**. _____

j) Circle one example of a fermata. Label it fermata.

UltimateMusicTheory.com © Copyright 2013 Gloryland Publishing. All Rights Reserved.

ULTIMATE MUSIC THEORY
PREPARATORY EXAM SET #2 - EXAM #3

Total Score: ___
100

1. a) Write the notes on the Grand Staff for the keys marked with a ☺. Use whole notes.
   b) Name the notes.
   c) Draw a line from each note to the corresponding key on the keyboard (at the correct pitch).

/10

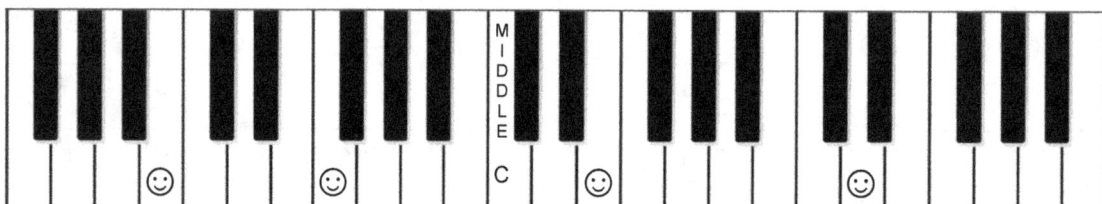

d) Name the following notes.

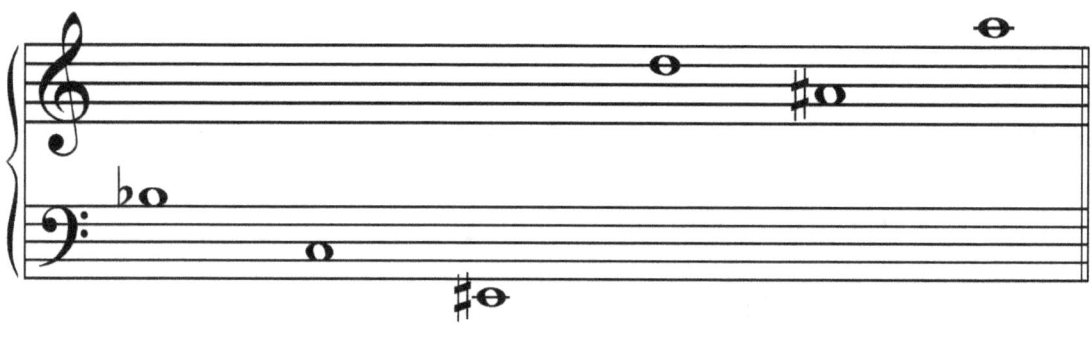

UltimateMusicTheory.com © Copyright 2013 Gloryland Publishing. All Rights Reserved.

ULTIMATE MUSIC THEORY
PREPARATORY EXAM SET #2 - EXAM #3

2. a) For each pair of notes, circle the note which sounds higher in pitch. Name the notes.

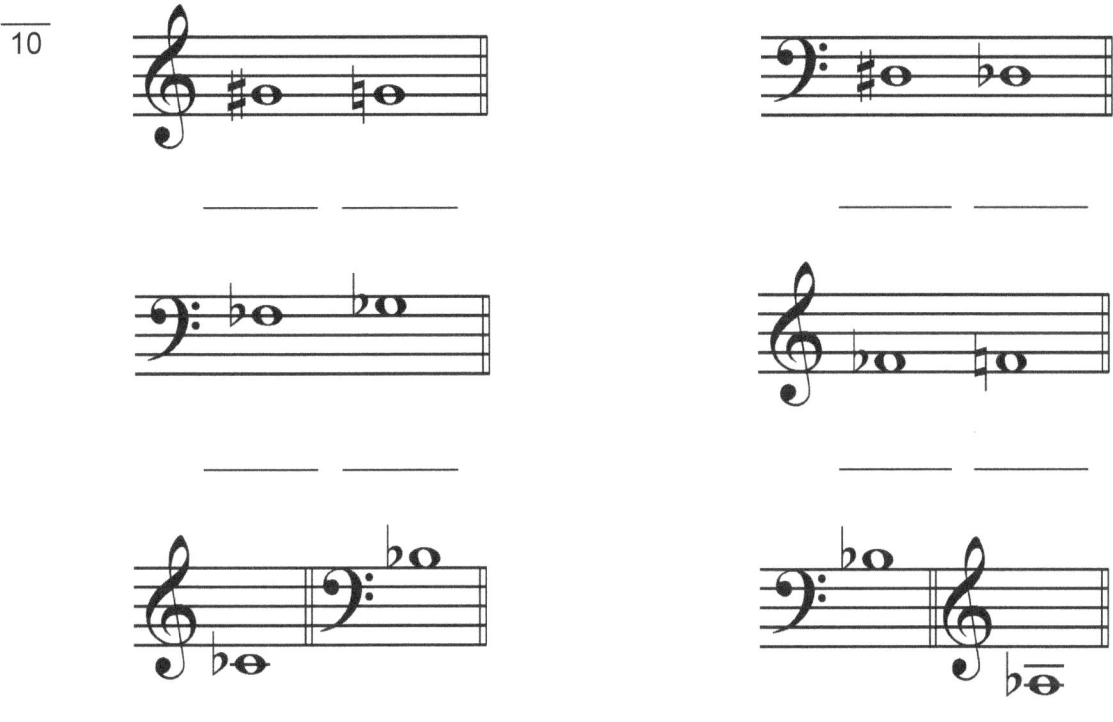

b) Beside each note, write the note that is one whole tone (whole step) lower. Use whole notes. Name the notes.

ULTIMATE MUSIC THEORY
PREPARATORY EXAM SET #2 - EXAM #3

3. a) Name the interval at each of the following letters. (Write the number size only.)

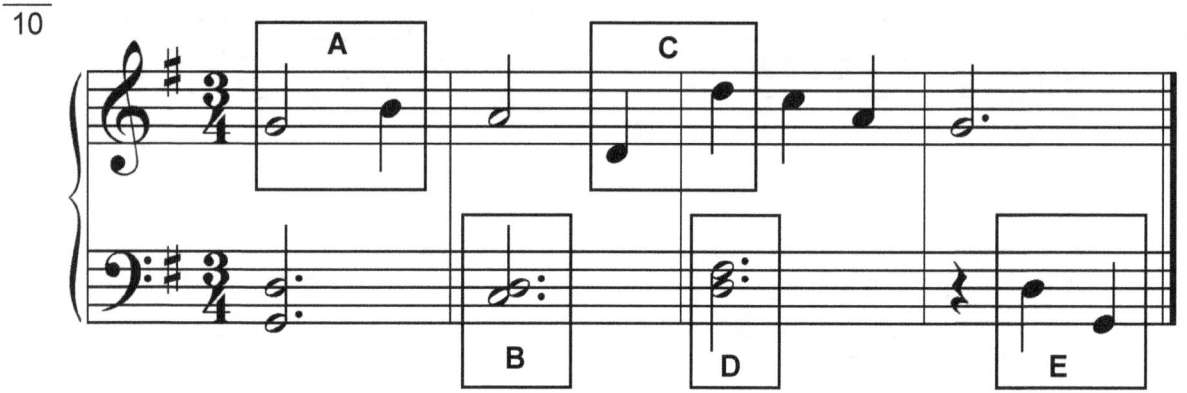

A _____

B _____

C _____

D _____

E _____

b) Write a note above each of the given notes to form the following harmonic intervals. Use whole notes.

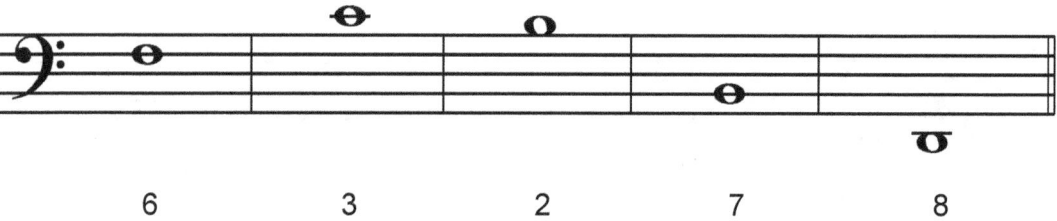

ULTIMATE MUSIC THEORY
PREPARATORY EXAM SET #2 - EXAM #3

4. Indicate if the rests in each measure are correct or incorrect by circling either CORRECT or INCORRECT.

CORRECT CORRECT CORRECT

INCORRECT INCORRECT INCORRECT

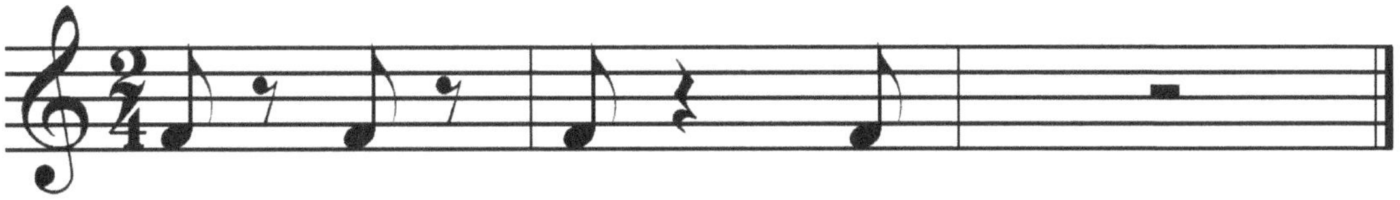

CORRECT CORRECT CORRECT

INCORRECT INCORRECT INCORRECT

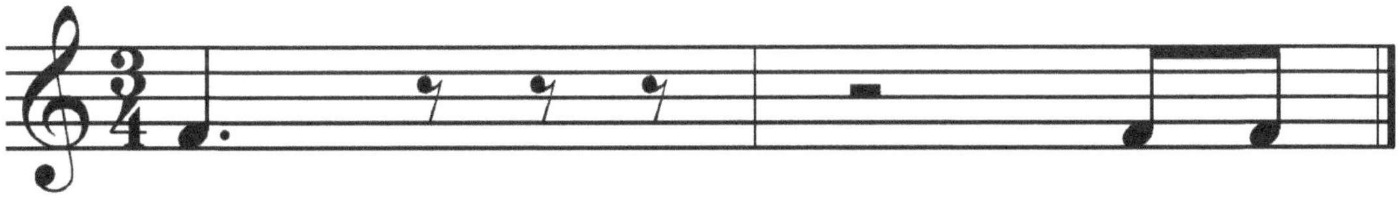

CORRECT CORRECT

INCORRECT INCORRECT

CORRECT CORRECT

INCORRECT INCORRECT

ULTIMATE MUSIC THEORY
PREPARATORY EXAM SET #2 - EXAM #3

5. a) Write the scale of F Major, descending (going down) one octave. Use accidentals instead of a Key Signature. Use whole notes. Circle one Tonic note. Label it as **I**.

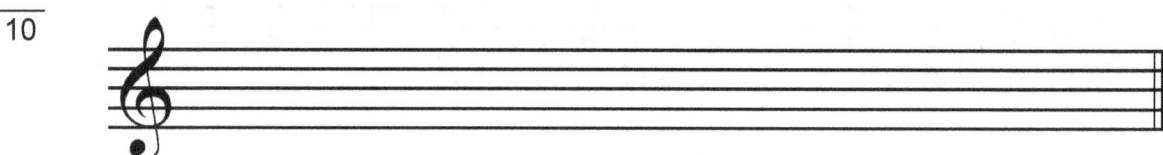

b) Write the scale of G Major, ascending (going up) one octave. Use accidentals instead of a Key Signature. Use whole notes. Circle one Tonic note. Label it as **I**.

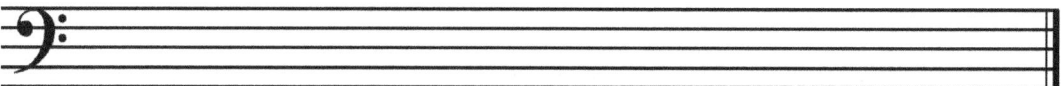

c) Write the scale of F Major, ascending (going up) one octave. Use a Key Signature. Use whole notes. Circle one Tonic note. Label it as **I**.

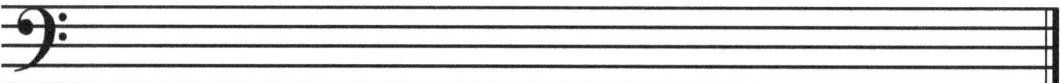

d) Write the scale of C Major, descending (going down) one octave. Use a Key Signature. Use whole notes. Circle one Tonic note. Label it as **I**.

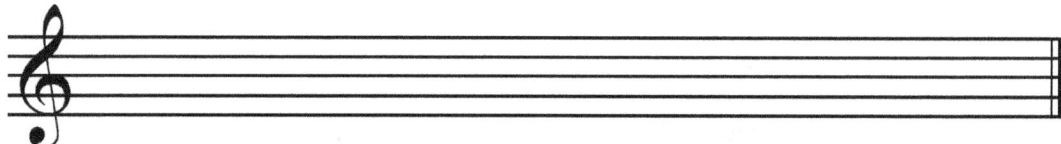

ULTIMATE MUSIC THEORY
PREPARATORY EXAM SET #2 - EXAM #3

6. Write the following solid (blocked) triads in Root Position on the Tonic note. Use whole notes.

___
10

F Major triad in the Bass Clef.
Use accidentals.

C Major triad in the Treble Clef.
Use a Key Signature.

G Major triad in the Bass Clef.
Use a Key Signature.

F Major triad in the Treble Clef.
Use a Key Signature.

C Major triad in the Bass Clef.
Use accidentals.

ULTIMATE MUSIC THEORY
PREPARATORY EXAM SET #2 - EXAM #3

7. a) Draw the following rests.

$\overline{10}$

   quarter rest =

   half rest =

   eighth rest =

   whole rest =

   b) Write the number of counts received when the notes are added together.

   example: ♪ ♪ ♪ = __1½__

    = _____

   ♩. ♪ = _____

    = _____

    = _____

   ♪ ♪ = _____

    = _____

ULTIMATE MUSIC THEORY
PREPARATORY EXAM SET #2 - EXAM #3

8. a) Add bar lines to complete the following rhythms.

b) Add the correct Time Signature below each bracket.

ULTIMATE MUSIC THEORY
PREPARATORY EXAM SET #2 - EXAM #3

9. Circle the correct term for each of the following signs or symbols.

Sign or Symbol	Term		
f	piano	or	forte
mp	mezzo piano	or	mezzo forte
<	crescendo	or	decrescendo
♩♩♩ (slur)	tie	or	slur
mf	mezzo piano	or	mezzo forte
♩. (staccato)	legato	or	staccato
>	crescendo	or	diminuendo
♩♩ (tie)	tie	or	slur
♭	sharp	or	flat
𝄐	fermata	or	natural

___
10

ULTIMATE MUSIC THEORY
PREPARATORY EXAM SET #2 - EXAM #3

10. Analyze the following excerpt of music by answering the questions below.

Minuet in F Major

G. F. Handel

Allegro

a) Name the title of this excerpt. _____

b) Explain the tempo of this excerpt. _____

c) Name the composer of this excerpt. _____

e) Add the Time Signature directly on the music.

d) Explain the dynamic sign in measure 1. _____

f) Name the notes at the letters   A: _____   B: _____

g) Explain the dynamic sign in measure 2. _____

h) Name the interval (number size only) at   C: _____   D: _____

i) Name the interval (number size only) at   E: _____   F: _____

j) How many times does the note B♭ appear in this excerpt? _____

UltimateMusicTheory.com © Copyright 2013 Gloryland Publishing. All Rights Reserved.

ULTIMATE MUSIC THEORY
PREPARATORY EXAM SET #2 - EXAM #4

Total Score: ___
100

1. a) Name the following notes.
   b) Draw a line from each note to the corresponding key on the keyboard (at the correct pitch).

___
10

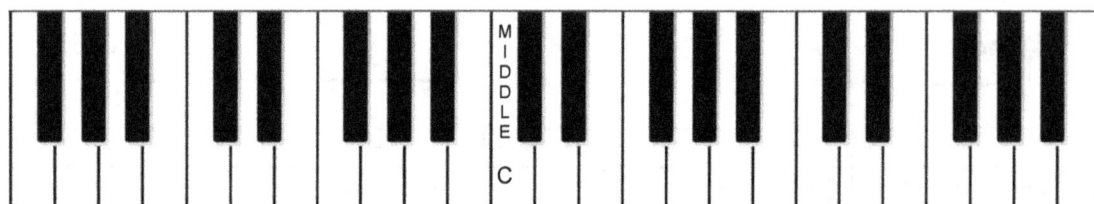

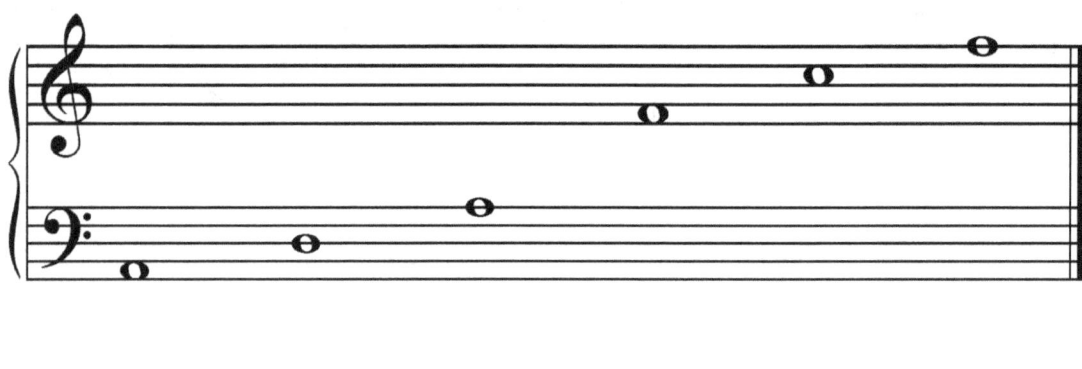

___ ___ ___ ___ ___

c) Write the following notes in the Treble Clef. Use dotted half notes.

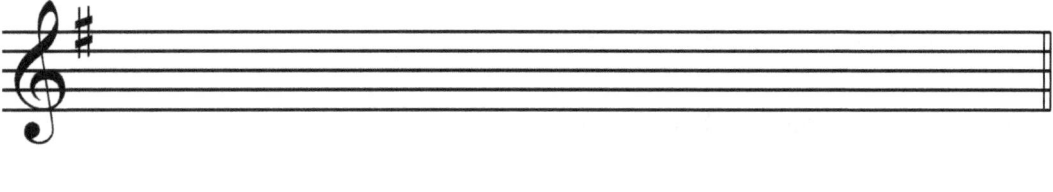

G   F#   F♮   F♭

UltimateMusicTheory.com © Copyright 2013 Gloryland Publishing. All Rights Reserved.

ULTIMATE MUSIC THEORY
PREPARATORY EXAM SET #2 - EXAM #4

2. a) For each pair of notes, circle the note which sounds higher in pitch. Name the notes.

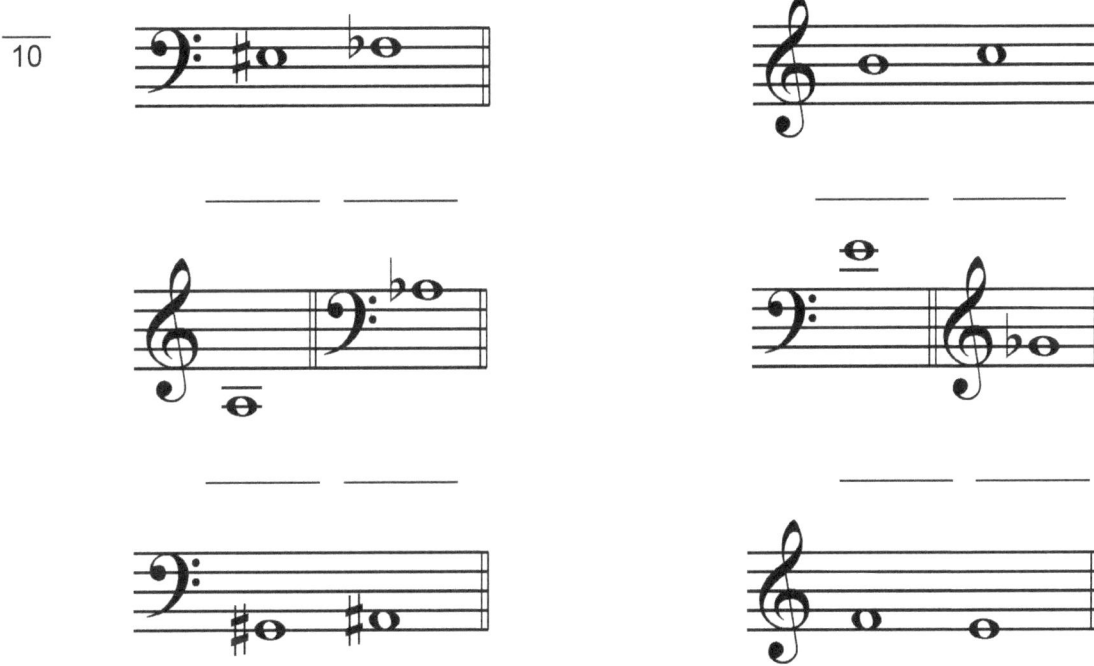

b) Indicate whether the distance between the notes in each measure is a semitone (half step) or a whole tone (whole step) by circling either SEMITONE or WHOLE TONE.

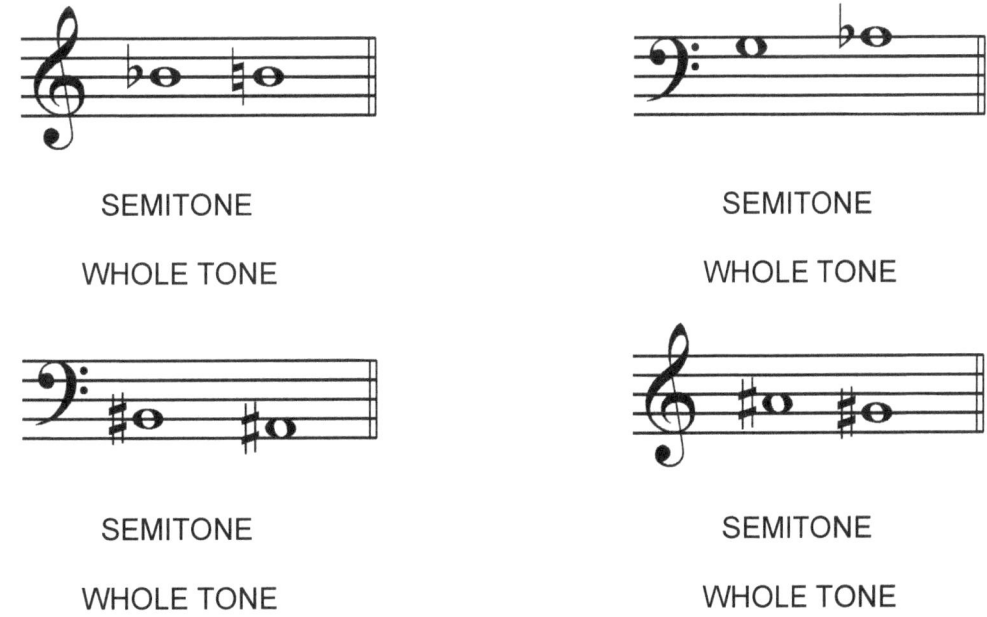

SEMITONE   SEMITONE

WHOLE TONE   WHOLE TONE

SEMITONE   SEMITONE

WHOLE TONE   WHOLE TONE

ULTIMATE MUSIC THEORY
PREPARATORY EXAM SET #2 - EXAM #4

3. a) Name each of the following harmonic intervals. (Write the number size only.)

b) Write a note above each of the given notes to form the following melodic intervals. Use half notes.

4. Add rests below each bracket to complete each measure.

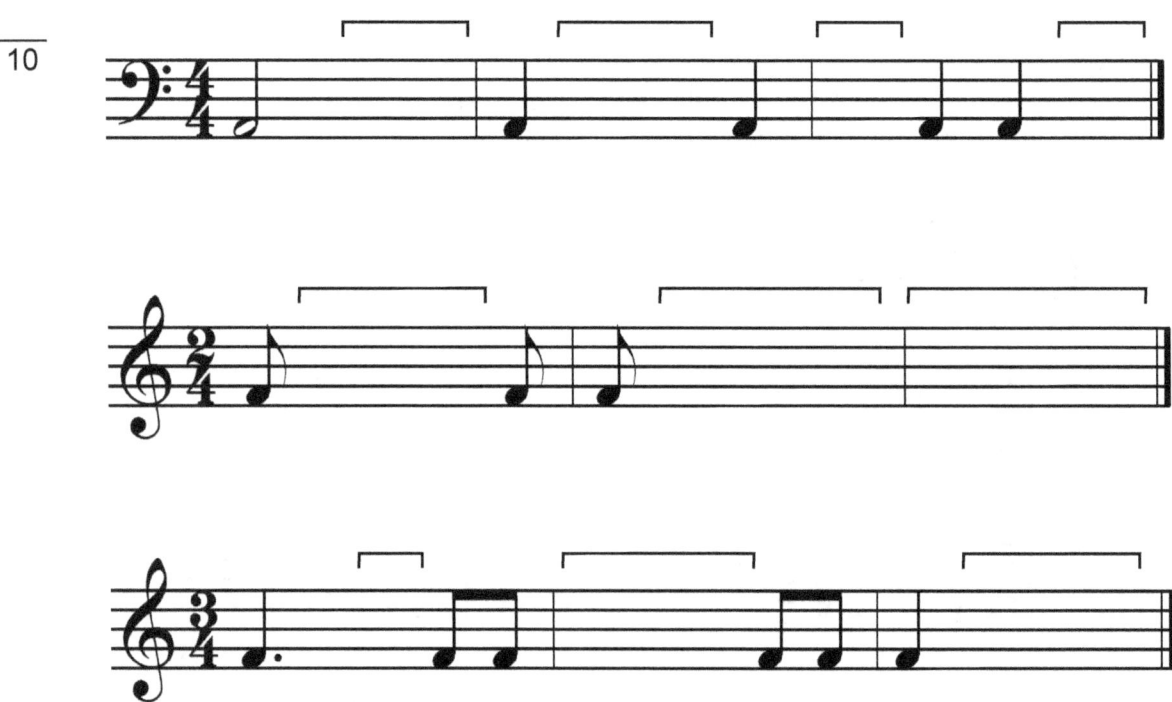

ULTIMATE MUSIC THEORY
PREPARATORY EXAM SET #2 - EXAM #4

5. a) Write the scale of G Major, descending (going down) one octave. Use accidentals instead of a Key Signature. Use whole notes. Circle one Tonic note. Label it as **I**.

10

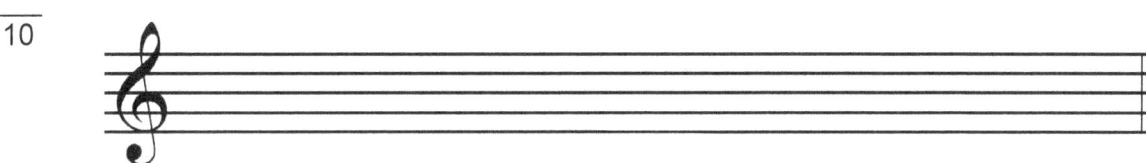

b) Write the scale of F Major, ascending (going up) one octave. Use accidentals instead of a Key Signature. Use whole notes. Circle one Tonic note. Label it as **I**.

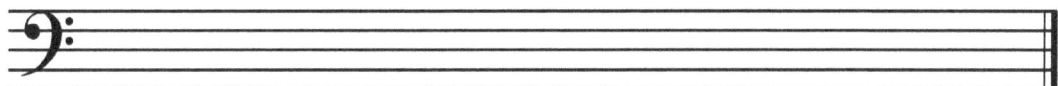

c) Write the scale of C Major, ascending (going up) one octave. Use a Key Signature. Use whole notes. Circle one Tonic note. Label it as **I**.

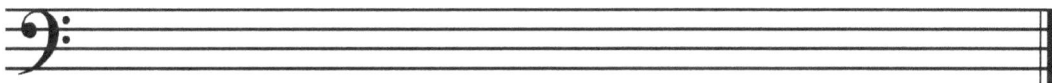

d) Write the scale of F Major, descending (going down) one octave. Use a Key Signature. Use whole notes. Circle one Tonic note. Label it as **I**.

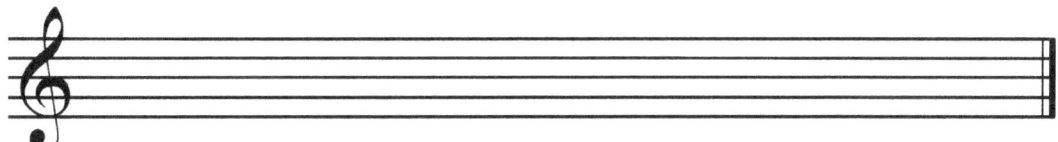

ULTIMATE MUSIC THEORY
PREPARATORY EXAM SET #2 - EXAM #4

6. Match each triad name with the correct triad.

__10__ G Major Triad, Broken, _____   a)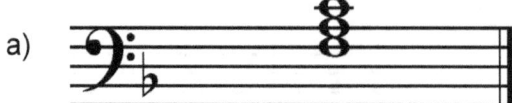
in the Bass Clef

G Major Triad, Solid, _____   b)
in the Treble Clef

F Major Triad, Solid, _____   c)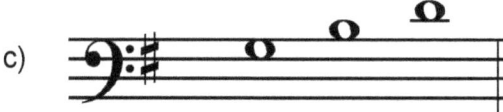
in the Bass Clef

C Major Triad, Broken, _____   d)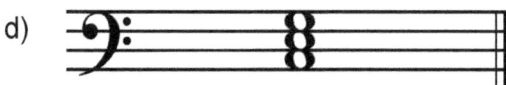
in the Treble Clef

C Major Triad, Solid, _____   e)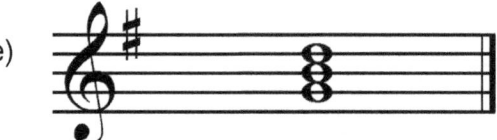
in the Bass Clef

ULTIMATE MUSIC THEORY
PREPARATORY EXAM SET #2 - EXAM #4

7. a) Name the following rests. Do not use abbreviations.

b) Write the number of counts received when the rests are added together.

example: ▬ 𝄾 𝄾 = __3__

𝄾 𝄾 = _____

𝄽 𝄾 = _____

𝄽 𝄽 𝄽 𝄽 = _____

𝄽 ▬ = _____

▬ ▬ = _____

▬ 𝄽 𝄽 = _____

ULTIMATE MUSIC THEORY
PREPARATORY EXAM SET #2 - EXAM #4

8. a) Add bar lines to complete the following rhythms.

b) Add the correct Time Signature below each bracket.

ULTIMATE MUSIC THEORY
PREPARATORY EXAM SET #2 - EXAM #4

9. Circle the correct definition for each of the following terms.

$\dfrac{}{10}$

Term	Definition		
legato	smooth	or	slow
mezzo forte	moderately soft	or	moderately loud
crescendo	becoming louder	or	becoming softer
ritardando	slowing down gradually	or	becoming faster
largo	very smooth	or	very slow
moderato	fast	or	at a moderate tempo
decrescendo	becoming louder	or	becoming softer
piano	soft	or	loud
slur	play the notes legato	or	a unit of musical time
fermata	detached	or	hold the note or rest longer than the written value

UltimateMusicTheory.com © Copyright 2013 Gloryland Publishing. All Rights Reserved.

ULTIMATE MUSIC THEORY
PREPARATORY EXAM SET #2 - EXAM #4

10. Analyze the following excerpt of music by answering the questions below.

Minuet in G Major

G. F. Handel

Moderato

mp   *cresc.*

a) Name the title of this excerpt. _____

b) Explain the tempo of this excerpt. _____

c) Add the Time Signature directly on the music.

e) Name the Key of this excerpt. _____

d) Explain the dynamic sign in measure 1. _____

f) Name the notes at the letters **A**: _____ **B**: _____

g) Is the curved line in measure 2 a tie or a slur? _____

h) Name the intervals at the letters **C**: _____ **D**: _____

i) How many times does the note F# appear in this excerpt? _____

j) What is the highest note in this piece? _____

ULTIMATE MUSIC THEORY EXAM SERIES

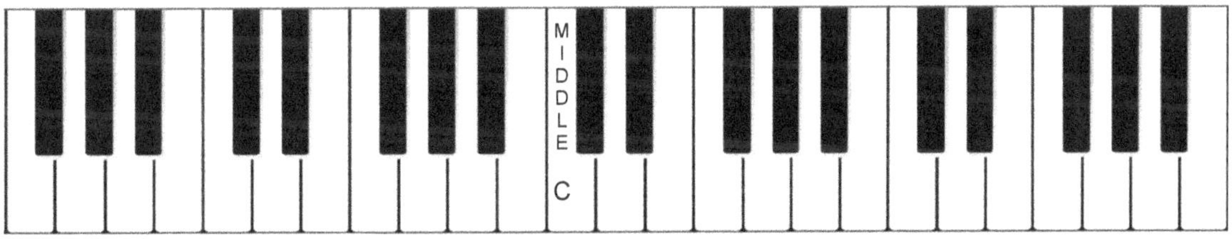

UltimateMusicTheory.com © Copyright 2013 Gloryland Publishing. All Rights Reserved.

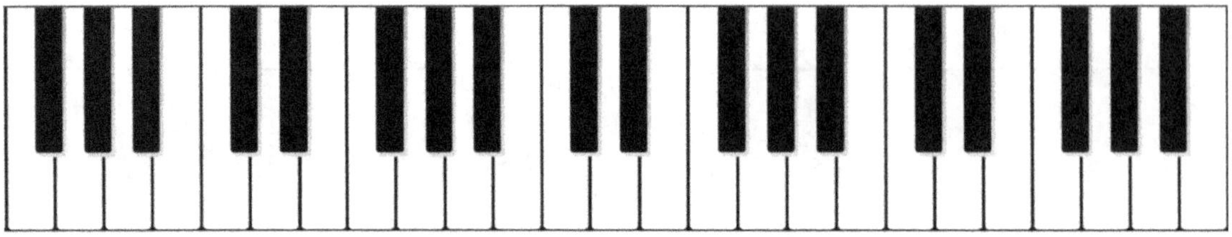

ULTIMATE MUSIC THEORY EXAM SERIES

UltimateMusicTheory.com © Copyright 2013 Gloryland Publishing. All Rights Reserved.

ULTIMATE MUSIC THEORY EXAM SERIES

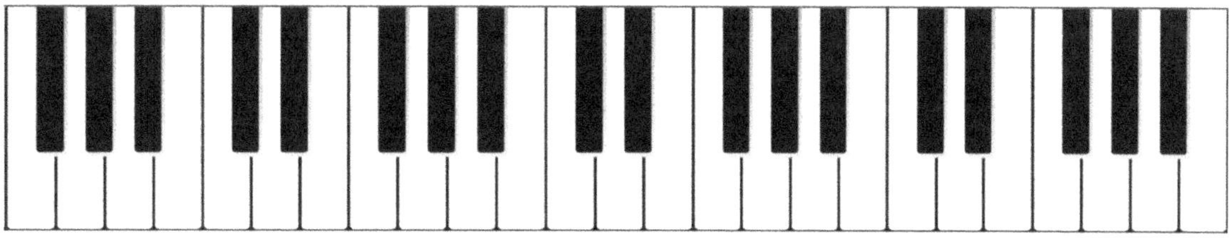

 **Workbooks, Exams, Answers, Online Courses, App & More!**

A Proven Step-by-Step System to Learn Theory Faster - from Beginner to Advanced.

Innovative techniques designed to develop a complete understanding of music theory, to enhance sight reading, ear training, creativity, composition and musical expression.

All UMT Series have matching Answer Books!

The UMT Rudiments Series - Beginner A, Beginner B, Beginner C, Prep 1, Prep 2, Basic, Intermediate, Advanced & Complete (All-In-One)

♪ 12 Lessons, Review Tests, and a Final Exam to develop confidence
♪ Music Theory Guide & Chart for fast and easy reference of theory concepts
♪ 80 Flashcards for fun drills to dramatically increase retention & comprehension

Rudiments Exam Series - Preparatory, Basic, Intermediate & Advanced

♪ 8 Exams plus UMT Tips on How to Score 100% on Theory Exams

Each Rudiments Workbook correlates to a Supplemental Workbook.

The UMT Supplemental Series - Prep Level, Level 1, Level 2, Level 3, Level 4, Level 5, Level 6, Level 7, Level 8 & Complete (All-In-One) Level

♪ Form & Analysis and Music History - Composers, Eras & Musical Styles
♪ Melody Writing using ICE - Imagine, Compose & Explore
♪ 12 Lessons, Review Tests, Final Exam and 80 Flashcards for quick study

Supplemental Exam Series - Level 5, Level 6, Level 7 & Level 8

♪ 8 Exams to successfully prepare for nationally recognized Theory Exams

UMT Online Courses, Music Theory App & More

♪ UMT Certification Course, Teachers Membership & Elite Educator Program
♪ Ultimate Music Theory App correlates to the Rudiments Workbooks
♪ Free Resources - Teachers Guide, Music Theory Blogs, videos & downloads

Go To: **UltimateMusicTheory.com**

www.ingramcontent.com/pod-product-compliance
Lightning Source LLC
Chambersburg PA
CBHW081736100526
44591CB00016B/2631